ALEXANDER VANDEGRIFT AS MARINE CORPS COMMANDANT

W0038117

UNITED STATES MARINE AT GUADALCANAL

World War II Comix
presents

RAIDERS, DESTROYERS & BANZAI CHARGES

GUADALCANAL

HAD IT ALL!

75TH Anniversary Remembrance

Written by: JAY WERTZ   Illustrated by: SEAN CARLSON

Publisher: Bill Breidenstine • Front Cover: Helle Urban
Art Direction & Lettering: Kevin Johnson
Ad Designer: Barb Justice • Printing: Caskey Group, York, PA

Available in Digital Format: **www.worldwariicomix.com**
Copyright 2018 - Monroe Publications
All Rights Reserved.

JAPANESE SOLDIER AT GUADALCANAL

REAR ADMIRAL RAIZO TANAKA, JAPANESE IMPERIAL NAVY

Strategic victories in the Battles of the Coral Sea and Midway enabled the United States to take the initiative against Japan while still preparing to put U. S. forces in action in the European Theater.

The Japanese were persistent in carrying out their plans. Despite losses at Midway, Imperial forces continued to build Pacific bases to launch future attacks. This included building a new airfield on Guadalcanal, in the southern Solomon Islands.

Navy chief Admiral Ernest J. King knew the Solomon Islands must be invaded.

His army and air force colleagues in Washington were preparing for the coming invasion of North Africa, the first American offensive in the defeat Germany first policy. So the Marine Corps, a force in the U. S. Navy, was designated to begin the Solomons ground campaign.

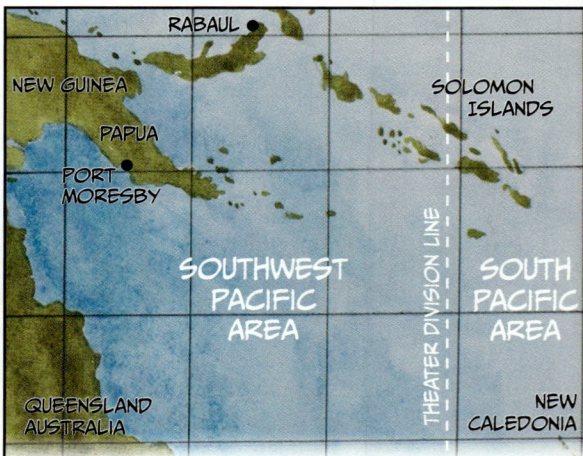

RABAUL
NEW GUINEA
SOLOMON ISLANDS
PAPUA
PORT MORESBY
SOUTHWEST PACIFIC AREA
THEATER DIVISION LINE
SOUTH PACIFIC AREA
QUEENSLAND AUSTRALIA
NEW CALEDONIA

Army Chief of Staff George Marshall was in full support of King's plan. To ease the coming operation, named *Watchtower*, the War Department redrew the theater division line, putting Guadalcanal in the sector assigned to Pacific Fleet commander Chester W. Nimitz.

Admiral Nimitz created a new South Pacific area under Rear Admiral Robert Ghormley, headquartered at a growing U. S. Navy base in Nouméa, New Caledonia.

Gen. MacArthur's SW Pacific command was tasked with stopping the Japanese advance in Papua, New Guinea.

After Coral Sea, Japanese strategy for taking Port Moresby changed from a navy campaign to an army advance over the Owen Stanley Mountains.

The United States Marines had a proud tradition as an elite force dating back to November 10, 1775, when the Continental Congress voted to raise two battalions of Continental Marines.

The Marines were the U. S. Navy's security and land combat force. In the early 19th century, they fought actions against enemies of the United States from Mexico to the Barbary Coast of Africa.

In July 1941, the Marines replaced British combat troops in the occupation of Iceland, to protect the neutral country from a German takeover. Fourth Regiment Marines stationed at Shanghai protected American interests in China.

In the first days of the war, the 4th Regiment left China for the Philippines. They fought the Japanese in a brave attempt to protect the last American bastion, Corregidor, and were then forced to surrender with the rest of the Allied forces.

After Pearl Harbor there was a flood of new Marine recruits. From boot camps in the Carolinas, as well as from bases in Virginia and Cuba, Marines traveled west across the heart of the United States to California embarkation points. At San Diego, recruits from the Western States became Marines.

In boot camp new recruits underwent rigorous physical, mental and emotional training to mold them into the finest quality fighting men in the elite tradition of the Marine Corps.

Edwin Cole Bearss from Montana was one of those recruits who reported to San Diego Marine Corps Recruiting Depot. Upon graduation, he participated in the boot camp tradition of presenting his drill instructor with a watch.

In West Coast ports Marines boarded transports - many of them leased or converted passenger liners - to cross the Pacific. Some were aboard USN ships that were summoned from the Atlantic and passed through the Panama Canal. On these voyages most of the young men crossed the equator for the first time.

They were initiated in the traditional King Neptune's ceremony, where they passed from being "pollywogs" to becoming "shellbacks."

After trips ranging up to a month, sometimes delayed by roundabout routes to avoid submarine hazards, the Marines arrived in South Pacific ports, including Nouméa, New Caledonia.

Upon reaching these South Seas camps, the Marines participated in amphibious training in preparation for landing in enemy territory. Weighed down with all their gear, they practiced climbing down rope nets into landing craft.

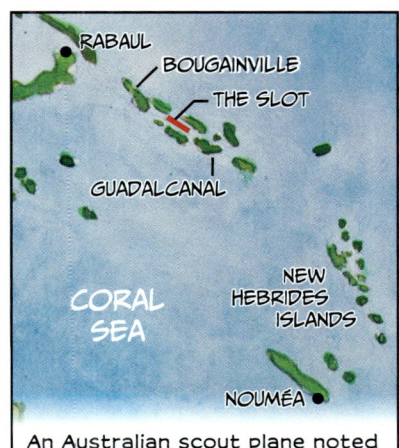

An Australian scout plane noted rapid Japanese progress in building the Guadalcanal airfield. Determined to prevent the field from becoming operational, American leaders pressed for an early invasion date, which was set as August 7, 1942.

In high level meetings from Washington to Pearl Harbor, Australia, and New Caledonia, details of *Operation Watchtower* were worked out. The 1st Marine Division, under Major General Alexander Vandegrift, was selected as the principal landing force.

Under the command of Vice Admiral Frank Jack Fletcher, a carrier task force took to sea to guard the Expeditionary Force of transports and other ships under Rear Admiral Richmond Kelly Turner.

Beginning at sunrise on August 7, high level B-17 and B-26 bombers of the U. S. Army Air Force hit Guadalcanal, Tulagi and other islands in the southern Solomons.

Anxious Marines waited on deck as the islands of Guadalcanal, Florida, Tulagi and Gavutu grew larger in their view.

Two rifle regiments of the 1st Marine Division, the 5th and the 1st, made up the assault wave.

They began the last leg of their journey to Guadalcanal in landing craft and amphibious tractors.

U. S. and Australian cruisers and destroyers shelled the islands just before the Marines landed.

Across the channel from Guadalcanal, Marines landed on Tulagi, at a location designated Beach Blue. Earlier, a small covering force landed on Florida Island.

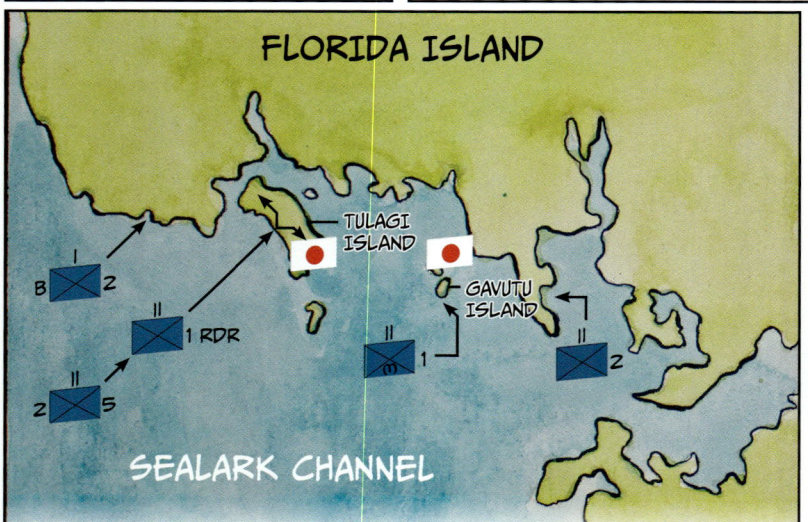

FLORIDA ISLAND

TULAGI ISLAND

GAVUTU ISLAND

B | 2

1 RDR

2 | 5

1

2

SEALARK CHANNEL

These smaller islands, assaulted by Marines of the 2nd & 5th Regiments, 1st Raiders and the Parachute Battalion, had to be taken because the Japanese headquarters and most of their supplies and men were here.

The 1st Raider Battalion Marines were specially trained for quick strikes and commando tactics.

An attack on Gavutu & Tanambogo, two small islands connected by a man-made causeway, was especially difficult. Navy warplanes aided the attackers.

On Tulagi, Marines blasted the Japanese out of caves and dugouts. When the fighting ended on August 8, all but three of the defenders were killed. A handful of Japanese escaped to Florida Island.

On Guadalcanal Island, the 5th Regiment Marines landed at 0910 on a desolate stretch of sand designated as Beach Red.

The Japanese did not contest the landing and the 1st and 5th Regiments quickly established a beachhead. Early in the afternoon, twin-engine "Betty" bombers arrived over Guadalcanal. They ignored the Marines on the beach and attacked Admiral Turner's transport force in Sealark Channel.

U. S. carrier planes and antiaircraft fire drove off the attackers, who destroyed the transport ship *George F. Elliot*. The threat of more aerial attacks pushed all hands to speed up the unloading process.

At 1100, the 1st Regiment landed on the beach.

They passed through the lines of the 5th Regiment and headed inland. The 5th Regiment headed west toward Lunga Point. By day's end both regiments had advanced about a mile.

On the morning of August 8, the transports continued to unload their cargos. Due to the daylong fighting on the other side of the channel, the Tulagi force did not receive its first supplies until the 8th.

Also on August 8, a 1st Marine Regiment battalion overran the airfield under construction and took custody of a few Korean laborers.

Japanese sailors and laborers withdrew to Kukum village, where they fought a short skirmish with a 5th Regiment battalion before fleeing into the jungle, leaving valuable supplies.

Coastwatchers in the Solomon Islands often provided early warnings of Japanese movements.

But none reported southbound cruisers in "the Slot" on August 8. Discovered during air searches, sketchy information led to an incorrect assessment of this force headed for Guadalcanal under Admiral Mikawa.

At 1800 Turner received notice of the enemy force, but believed those ships were planning an air strike the next day.

He called his top commanders together that night to schedule withdrawal of the transports. Just after midnight Mikawa's cruisers penetrated the American radar screen and attacked the Allied warships patrolling on both sides of Savo Island.

Launching torpedoes and firing their big guns, the Japanese fatally damaged four Allied cruisers in less than an hour.

They all sunk or were scuttled after dawn. More than 1,000 Allied sailors were killed in the Battle of Savo Island. But fearing aerial retaliation, Mikawa withdrew without attacking the transports.

With the withdrawal of the carrier force on the 8th, and the loss of cruisers of the Screening Force overnight...

Turner ordered the transports to leave as soon as repairs were made to damaged vessels. By 1830 the last ships departed Sealark Channel, leaving 17,000 men with limited supplies and equipment.

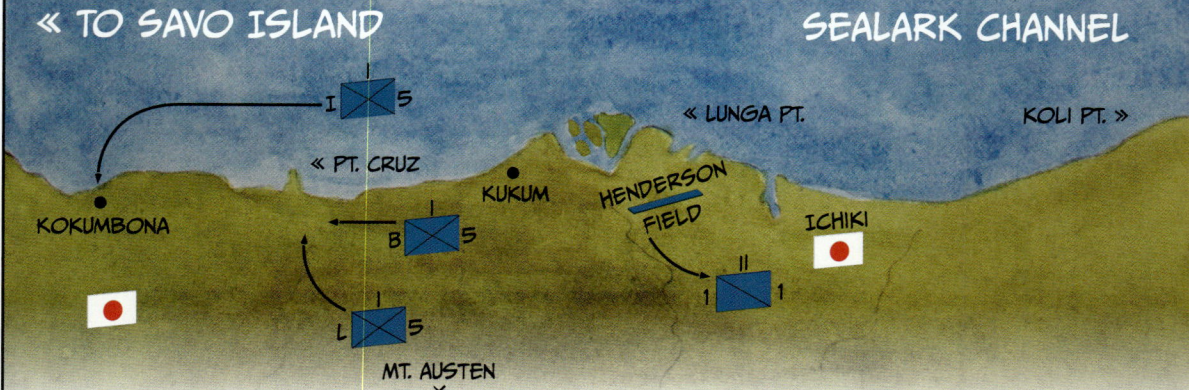

With the scant resources they brought ashore, augmented by materials and equipment the Japanese abandoned, navy and Marine construction units worked to complete the airfield. It was named Henderson Field after Marine pilot and squadron leader Lofton Henderson, who was killed in the Battle of Midway. A patchwork perimeter was set up on Lunga Point to protect the airfield. On August 19, General Vandegrift ordered a one-day strike west across the Matanikau River toward the village of Kokumbona. Intelligence data revealed most of the Japanese on the island had gathered there. Meanwhile, the Japanese were landing troops east of the airfield to prepare for their first offensive.

On August 19 the first planes to be based at Henderson Field landed.

These Wildcat fighters and scout bombers formed the first two Marine squadrons to be based at Henderson. Army Air Force P-400 pursuit planes, and some dive bombers loaned from carrier *Enterprise*, soon joined them.

While Marines were invading the Solomons, the 2nd Raider Battalion landed from submarines on Makin Atoll in the Central Pacific.

The objective of these highly trained commandos was to divert Japanese attention from Guadalcanal by causing havoc much closer to Japan.

Within a few days of the American landing, the British leader on Guadalcanal, Captain Martin Clemens, emerged from hiding and offered the services of his Solomon Islands Defense Force. These native islanders proved very valuable as scouts and spies.

In the early morning hours of August 21 the first Japanese reinforcements to arrive, called the Ichiki Force, attacked Lunga Point.

With fixed bayonets, they charged across the Ilu River against the 2nd Battalion of the 1st Marines. Using machine guns and artillery, the Marines inflicted heavy losses on Ichiki's men.

Ichiki attacked prematurely while the rest of the Japanese 35th Brigade was being shuttled to Guadalcanal on the "Tokyo Express," fast destroyers and cruisers embarking troops at Rabaul and Bougainville to challenge the Marines holding Lunga Point.

Vandegrift ordered riflemen, supported by light tanks, to venture beyond the defensive perimeter when daylight came.

The Ichiki Force was wiped out and the first threat to the airfield was defeated. But lack of supplies and Japanese air strikes still handicapped the Marines.

In support of the landing of the 35th Brigade, Admiral Yamamoto assembled ships of the Combined Fleet with the naval forces based at Rabaul. He hoped to draw the Pacific Fleet carrier force into an engagement. On August 23, a USN search plane discovered the large Japanese naval force.

After the August 7 landing, Adm. Fletcher had been keeping his TF-61 southeast of Guadalcanal. He moved toward the Japanese concentration with *Saratoga* and *Enterprise*, while *Wasp* was held back. The Battle of the Eastern Solomons began on August 24 with TF-61 dive bombers attacking and sinking *Ryujo* of the aptly named Diversion Group.

While this was happening, Admiral Kondo's planes from the Striking Group attacked TF-61. *Enterprise* was badly damaged and Fletcher withdrew, but the Japanese lost many planes. On August 25, B-17 bombers and Marine dive bombers attacked the Transport Group. The Japanese cancelled the landing.

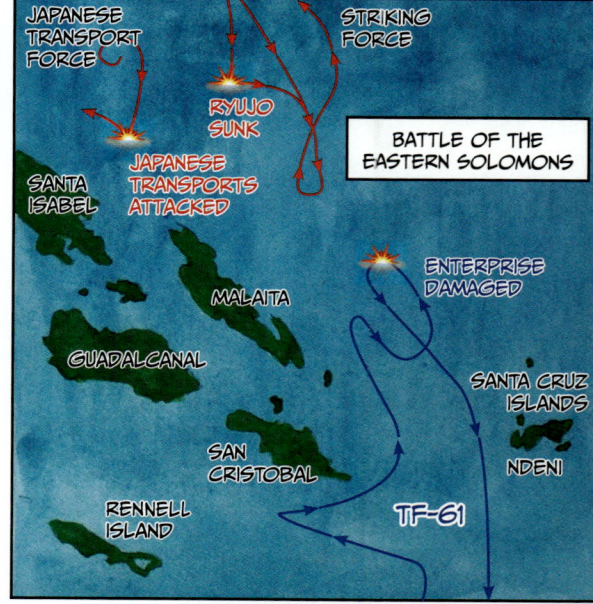

JAPANESE TRANSPORT FORCE

STRIKING FORCE

RYUJO SUNK

JAPANESE TRANSPORTS ATTACKED

BATTLE OF THE EASTERN SOLOMONS

SANTA ISABEL

MALAITA

ENTERPRISE DAMAGED

GUADALCANAL

SANTA CRUZ ISLANDS

SAN CRISTOBAL

NDENI

RENNELL ISLAND

TF-61

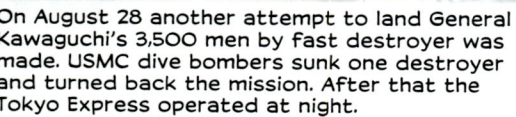

On August 28 another attempt to land General Kawaguchi's 3,500 men by fast destroyer was made. USMC dive bombers sunk one destroyer and turned back the mission. After that the Tokyo Express operated at night.

Admiral Ghormley continued to send supplies to Guadalcanal by ship.

Fletcher's two remaining carriers guarded the supply convoys and flew search missions. On August 31, a Japanese sub attack damaged *Saratoga*, putting it out of action for weeks alongside *Enterprise*.

In the Southwest Pacific Area, the Japanese continued their overland campaign to attack the airdrome at Port Moresby.

Australian forces were sent up the Kokoda Trail to meet them. Imperial General Headquarters had not yet accepted that the pivotal campaign was at Guadalcanal.

Rested troops, the 1st Raider and Parachute battalions, arrived from Tulagi.

On September 8, they landed east of Lunga Point at the village of Tasimboko, where they overran a camp. They then ran into strong resistance from seasoned army infantry. This raid told Gen. Vandegrift that a large number of Japanese reinforcements had landed on Guadalcanal.

In the beginning of September, while the Marines worked to build and strengthen their defensive perimeter, the Japanese bombed Henderson Field every day at noon. They also sent a noisy night bomber the Marines called "Washing Machine Charlie" to harass the troops.

The Japanese continued to land reinforcements on Guadalcanal at night.

By the middle of the month Clemens' scouts reported 7,000 Japanese on Guadalcanal. These soldiers, called the Kawaguchi Force, began to cut a trail inland around Henderson Field.

Kawaguchi's three battalions positioned themselves in the jungle along the Lunga River, between Henderson Field and Mount Austen.

With his two regiments holding the coast and river crossings, Vandegrift sent Col. Merritt Edson's 1st Raiders, the Parachute Battalion and other small units to defend a long ridge that led to Henderson Field. Beginning on the night of September 12, the Kawaguchi Force made repeated attacks on the ridge. The Marine line bent, but never broke and by the 14th all attempts by the Japanese to reach the airfield over "Bloody Ridge" had failed.

Of the 2,000 Japanese who attacked Bloody Ridge, at least 600 were killed. The shaken survivors retreated; some to the east, some west along the base of Mount Austen.

Ghormley and Turner decided it was time to bring the 7th Marine Regiment from Samoa, with more supplies and additional air crews.

But the mission to greatly bolster Guadalcanal's defense had a cost; *Wasp* was sunk and battleship *North Carolina* was damaged by submarine torpedoes.

The 7th saw action almost immediately. On September 23, the 1st Battalion, under Lieutenant Colonel Lewis B. "Chesty" Puller, along with the 1st Raiders and 2nd Battalion, 5th Marines, were ordered across the Matanikau River. This advance broke down almost immediately amid heavy casualties.

Part of the 1st Battalion, 7th Marines landed west of the river by boat and were cut off. Puller used the guns of the destroyer-transport *Ballard* to occupy the enemy, allowing his men to escape in landing craft.

The Marines attacked across the Matanikau again on October 7 and 9.

The results were better for the Americans. Marine artillery backed the advances. Puller's men, circling inland and advancing toward the coast, wiped out a large number of Japanese soldiers trapped in a deep ravine.

After this action, the Marines were able to build fortified artillery positions aimed across the Matanikau in preparation for the next big offensive.

At their base in Truk, Japanese leaders planned their major counteroffensive to retake Guadalcanal.

Troops were summoned from other regions to insure success. General Hyakutake, 17th Army Commander, took charge of the new campaign to recapture Guadalcanal in the third week of October.

The Americans were also taking steps to insure success. A late September convoy brought the first U. S. army infantry unit to Guadalcanal, the 164th Regiment. Transports also unloaded much needed combat vehicles, aviation crews and supplies; then left with the 1st Raider Battalion on board.

In addition to enduring daily bombing, shelling and shortages, another problem rocked Guadalcanal's garrison - a steady increase in sick calls. Exposure to malaria and other diseases, a hostile environment and gunfire forced many men into medical stations or evacuation from the island.

While screening for the 164th Regiment convoy, Rear Admiral Norman Scott's Task Force 64 was alerted to Japanese ships in the Slot.

The three cruisers and two destroyer were tasked with shelling Henderson Field to prevent American planes from intercepting the next Tokyo Express run. Early on October 1, near Guadalcanal's northwest tip, Scott's cruisers and destroyers surprised the Japanese ships, sinking two and turning back the rest.

Satisfaction over victory in this naval Battle of Cape Esperance was short lived. Beginning at noon on October 13, Japanese planes, ground artillery and later ships shelled Henderson Field relentlessly. The campaign inflicted heavy damage and casualties. Marines simply called it "The Bombardment."

New in this action was the appearance of Japanese battleships. *Kongo* and *Haruna* brought the first 14-inch guns to bear on the U. S. positions.

Along with cruisers and destroyers they lined up in the channel to shell the Marines and everything they had built. Pesky American PT boats did little damage but their presence concerned Japanese Admiral Kurita enough to pull out early.

Though other Japanese ships arrived to continue the shelling over two nights, Imperial Navy leaders underestimated U.S. resources and resolve.

On October 15, U.S. Navy fighters, dive bombers and army B-17s attacked the heavily guarded Japanese transports unloading near Cape Esperance, destroying three and damaging the others.

Orders were cut for the newcomers to join Kawaguchi's remaining troops and attack north in two wings toward Lunga Point. Japanese engineers cut a new trail through the thick jungle on the back side of Mount Austen.

Vandegrift and his commanders knew when the Japanese landed on October 15 that a major attack was coming.

Marine and army units on the Lunga perimeter worked to strengthen their defenses, which now formed a complete belt around the airfields with an extension toward the Matanikau.

After artillery shelling and several patrols alerted Marines to a Japanese offensive brewing at the mouth of the Matanikau, nine Japanese medium tanks crossed the sandbar on October 23.

Marine artillery prevented their supporting infantry from crossing the river. The tanks were wiped out by cannon fire and a tracked tank destroyer.

Just after midnight on October 25, the Japanese 29th Regiment attacked alone because the right wing became lost in the dark and driving rain. Puller's regiment of Marines, aided by two battalions of the 164th, prevented a breakthrough during this attack and an attack by both wings the next night.

After dawn on October 25, the Japanese bombed Henderson Field with heavy artillery and planes. Some aircraft in the "Cactus Air Force," a name derived from a code word for Guadalcanal, avoided serious damage by being camouflaged. By the end of October, however, only 29 operational aircraft remained.

The three Japanese ground assaults, October 23-26, were uncoordinated and short on heavy weapons. They faced a determined American force in prepared positions, supported by artillery and covered by mobile reinforcements. Hyakutake's major counteroffensive was a costly failure.

LENGO CHANNEL

« PT. CRUZ

KUKUM

HQ

HENDERSON FIELD

FIGHTER STRIP

SUMIYOSHI FORCE 10-23

PERIMETER EXTENSION

LUNGA MARINE DEFENSE PERIMETER

3 — 164

MATANIKAU RIVER

LUNGA RIVER

OKA FORCE 10-25

— INFANTRY

— TANKS

— ARTILLERY

MT. AUSTEN

MARUYAMA FORCE 10-25 / 10-26

More than 1,500 dead Japanese lay just outside the lines on the southern slope of Bloody Ridge, a sad testament to the fanaticism of the attackers and the fortitude of the defenders.

Though the ground offensive was defeated, the heavy bombardment of Henderson Field salvaged some success for the Japanese in the October offensive. The campaign also produced another inconclusive sea battle which took place in open waters east of Guadalcanal.

In this contest called the Battle of the Santa Cruz Islands, U. S. carrier *Hornet* was relentlessly attacked and could not be saved. *Enterprise* was damaged. Two Japanese carriers were damaged and they sustained another critical loss of planes and pilots.

Damage to Henderson and the new grass Fighter Airstrip were quickly repaired. But fuel supplies were critically low even though improvised means, including flying aviation fuel to Guadalcanal in cargo planes, were employed. So B-17s on Solomon Islands missions had to be staged through Espiritu Santo instead.

Meanwhile Japanese soldiers landed at Koli Point east of the Lunga perimeter. Hyakutake considered using the area to establish a new Japanese airfield.

With a depleted enemy force in the beginning of November, Vandegrift ordered an operation to cross the Matanikau. A massive artillery barrage preceded the attack of various units under Col. Edson.

A battalion of the 7th Marines sent to Koli Point ran into stout resistance. Marine reinforcements were sent by landing craft. Eventually a number of the Japanese were forced into an inescapable pocket while the rest withdrew to the west.

The Marine 2nd Raiders followed the Makin Raid with another extraordinary mission.

In the second week of November the 8th Marines of the 2nd Marine Division landed on Guadalcanal.

Landing 33 miles east of Lunga at Aola Bay on November 4, the Raiders chased the Koli Point stragglers through the island's interior, killing many, before entering the Lunga Perimeter on December 4.

Also in the convoy were 155mm guns of the Marines 11th Regiment. The Guadalcanal veterans finally had cannons to compete with the largest Japanese artillery, which the Marines dubbed "Pistol Pete," and which were located west of the Matanikau River.

Despite the October ground war setback, Hyakutake and those above him were still committed to driving the Americans from Guadalcanal.

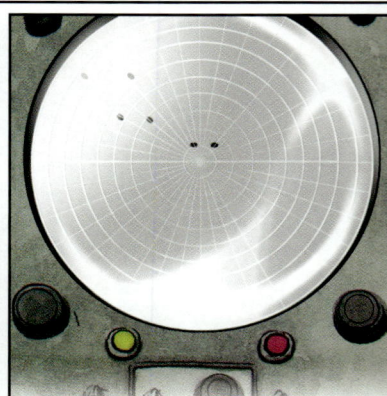

In early November Tokyo Express runs continued to bring in soldiers. But a vast reinforcement, supply and bombardment mission was desired and Admiral Yamamoto assembled the largest sea force yet to get it to Guadalcanal.

By November 1942 many U. S. Navy ships had radar and trained operators. Several radar equipped ships were in Admiral Daniel Callaghan's task group of cruisers and destroyers, supporting the transports bringing in the 182nd Infantry Regiment, USA.

Just after O145 on Friday the 13th, Callahan's column of eight destroyers and five cruisers steamed close enough to those radar blips east of Savo Island to start an all-out gunfight.

The lead destroyers and cruiser *Atlanta* crossed into the Japanese formation and paid dearly for doing so. American ships concentrated fire on the Japanese battleship *Hiei*, but *Hiei*, *Kirishima* and their destroyer escorts were firing searchlight-guided torpedoes and shells into the scattered American ships with great effect. With *Hiei* heavily damaged Japanese admiral Abe broke off the attack, but not before damaging every U. S. vessel but one and killing many sailors, including admirals Callahan and Scott.

Despite the pummeling they received, all but five of the American ships made it out of Ironbottom Sound. The Japanese incendiary shells, meant for Henderson Field, damaged the American ships topside, but spared their armor-plated hulls. Heavy cruiser *San Francisco*, light cruisers *Helena* and *Juneau* and three destroyers sailed away to the southeast after dawn. *Juneau* was torpedoed by the infamous sub *I-26* and sank. The fast moving column left behind many sailors who did not survive delayed search efforts.

Also left behind was *Hiei*, heavily damaged and sitting north of Savo Island. Admiral Halsey was sending everything he had into the Naval Battle of Guadalcanal, as this four-day action was called, including *Enterprise*, still undergoing repairs at sea. Some of "Big E's" planes, sent ahead to Henderson, were the first to discover wounded *Hiei*. On Friday afternoon they dropped deadly torpedoes into the battleship. Marine planes and B-17s finished off *Hiei*, which sunk that evening.

Minutes into Saturday, November 14, Admiral Mikawa's destroyers and cruisers arrived off Henderson Field when only PT boats were in range to oppose them.

The 37-minute shelling did not shut down Henderson Field; and more planes were damaged than destroyed. Marine aviation tech Constant Piccionelli and others pitched in to get the Cactus Air Force back in action.

As daylight arrived on the 14th American planes from *Enterprise*, Guadalcanal and Espiritu Santo pounced on Mikawa's warships going up the Slot.

A more important target was Raizo Tanaka's convoy of troop ships headed for Guadalcanal. Seven transports were destroyed by the mixed group of U. S. planes present, including fifteen B-17s, whose gunners shot down six Zeros.

By nightfall two U.S. battleships were approaching Guadalcanal under Rear Adm. Willis Lee. USS *Washington*, *South Dakota* and four destroyers were on a collision course with ships under Adm. Konda.

The U. S. destroyers took the brunt of Kondo's firepower just before midnight. *South Dakota* had electrical problems that limited its fighting ability, but *Washington* took the lead, fatally disabling battleship *Kirishima* and causing Kondo to withdraw.

The battleship clash and Kondo's withdrawal left Tanaka's transports and destroyers unprotected off Guadalcanal's coast.

Beaching the transports, Tanaka left after a fraction of the reinforcements who came down the Slot made it ashore. Daylight on November 15 brought planes from Guadalcanal and *Enterprise*; destroyer *Meade* and Marine artillery, all feasting on grounded Japanese ships, soldiers and supplies.

Even though the Naval Battle of Guadalcanal cost the U. S. a great number of ships and lives…

it put an end to Japanese naval efforts to retake Guadalcanal and control the skies over the island. But Hyakutake's units were not going to surrender. They would have to be eliminated or forced from the island.

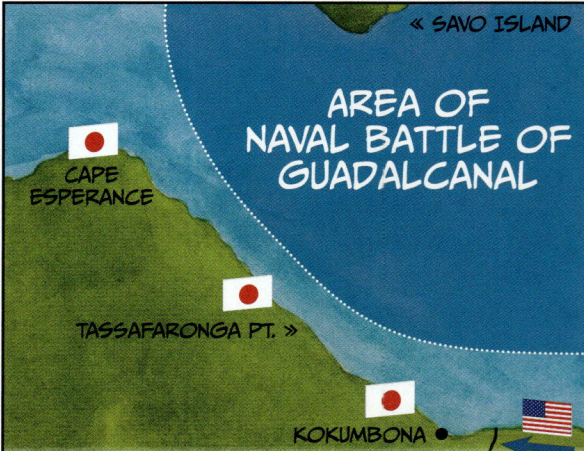

« SAVO ISLAND

AREA OF NAVAL BATTLE OF GUADALCANAL

CAPE ESPERANCE

TASSAFARONGA PT. »

KOKUMBONA ●

Encouraged by the naval victory, Vandegrift ordered the offensive west resumed on November 18. The going was tough for the two army regiments assigned to advance against the dug-in Japanese west of the Matanikau. After five days the drive was suspended, though some new ground was gained.

At the same time the tide was turning on Guadalcanal, Douglas MacArthur's command was gaining ground in Papua.

GIs were airlifted to a point on the peninsula that outflanked the Japanese on the Kokoda Trail. The enemy was forced into the restrictive enclaves of Buna and Gona on Papua's northern coast.

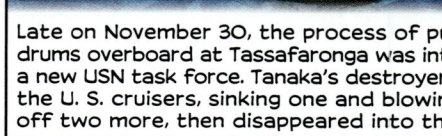

Adm. Tanaka was ordered to haul supplies down the Slot to Hyakutake's men, mostly gasoline drums filled with rice and lashed together on the decks of destroyers.

Late on November 30, the process of pushing the drums overboard at Tassafaronga was interrupted by a new USN task force. Tanaka's destroyers torpedoed the U. S. cruisers, sinking one and blowing the bows off two more, then disappeared into the night.

The 1st Marine Division, after four months of survival living and hard fighting, left Guadalcanal for rest in Australia about December 1. Gen. Vandegrift turned over command to Gen. Alexander Patch, who would lead two army divisions and the 2nd Marine Division to defeat or drive Japanese forces from Cactus.

Of the roughly 25,000 Japanese soldiers on Guadalcanal on December 1, most were huddled in jungle camps that hid them from American controlled skies. Limited in ammunition, food and medicine, the harsh jungle conditions caused greater suffering from disease than their enemy endured.

The first major operation undertaken by Gen. Patch was to clear the Japanese from Mt. Austen.

On December 17 two battalions of the 132nd Regiment began the trek into Mt. Austen's series of hills. In many places the rugged terrain and Japanese defensive positions slowed the advance, which didn't reach its goals until year's end after the 2nd Battalion was called up to help.

The strongest Japanese defensive positions on Guadalcanal was west of Mt. Austen's peak. The Gifu, named for a section of Honshu Island, was an array of interlocking log machine gun nests manned by 500 dedicated survivors of Col. Oka's command.

When the corps advance began on January 10, 1943, spearheaded by the 25th Division, USA and Marine 2nd Division, steep ridges covered most of the front. To aid the assaults on Japanese positions, Cactus fighters and dive bombers preceded the infantry.

As GIs moved to the jungles of western Guadalcanal, supply and medical aid became challenges. Native islanders were employed, air drops were arranged, and the versatile Jeep was used in the rugged ridge areas, including to evacuate the wounded.

While the 25th Division inched forward through the hills west of Mt. Austen...

the 2nd Marine Division tackled strong Japanese positions west of Point Cruz beginning on January 13. For the first time flame thrower teams were used to clear out Japanese emplacements. After five days, the Marines were ready to assault Kokumbona.

Despite progress inland, the Gifu still held out. From January 15-17 an army officer broadcast surrender appeals in Japanese to Gifu defenders. The idea was not successful.

Despite a heavy artillery bombardment and infantry assaults from all sides, resistance continued in the Gifu until January 22, when a USMC tank led GIs in capturing the stronghold.

Another buildup of ships in the Solomons had U.S. leaders suspecting a new reinforcement effort was in the works, but this activity was to cover the Japanese withdrawal from Guadalcanal.

Halsey countered with a navy show of force. These ships were introduced to a new Japanese night bombing technique, which resulted in the torpedoing of USS *Chicago* on January 29. A nearly suicidal air strike the next day sunk the venerable warship.

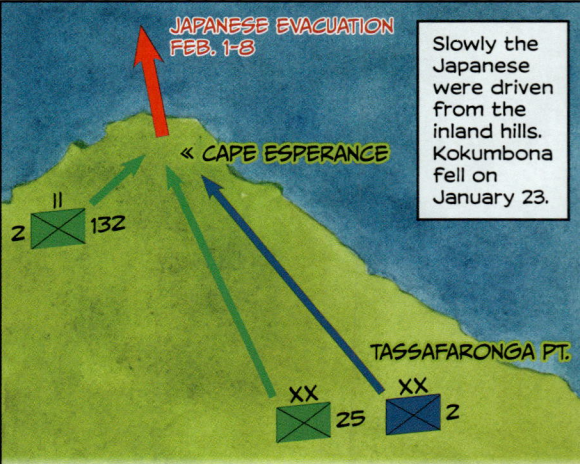

JAPANESE EVACUATION FEB. 1-8

« CAPE ESPERANCE

2 | II | 132

TASSAFARONGA PT.

XX 25   XX 2

Slowly the Japanese were driven from the inland hills. Kokumbona fell on January 23.

The 25th Division and 2nd Marines, supported by American artillery and Cactus planes, forced the Japanese to the northwest. To contain the retreating enemy, on February 1 boats took an army battalion to Guadalcanal's west coast.

On three separate nights beginning on February 1, Hyakutake's cornered survivors were plucked off Guadalcanal by destroyer. Fast moving American units battled a small Japanese rear guard of fresh troops, but the outcome was not in doubt.

With the knowledge of a job well done, American forces on Guadalcanal felt a deep sense of relief.

Soon, there were more battles to be fought before the Solomon Islands could effectively be taken out of the war. Guadalcanal, the first great American/Allied victory of the Pacific War, was the catalyst to driving Japan from the Pacific islands.

World War II Comix

presents

SEPARATED
BY
WAR

Written by **Jay Wertz**

Illustrated by **Benny Jordan**

MOE IS RIGHT. A MILE FROM THE CANOE THEY SEE A SURFACED U. S. NAVY SUBMARINE. JENSEN RECOGNIZES THE CRAFT FROM PEARL HARBOR. SUDDENLY, A LARGE SWELL GLIDES PAST THE SUB.

THE SUBMARINE IS USS *NAUTILUS*, ONE OF TWO ON THIS AMERICAN COMMANDO MISSION TO MAKIN. SUDDENLY THE BIG SUB GOES INTO A DIVE AND SUBMERGES.

JENSEN MOTIONS HIS FRIENDS TO GET THE CANOE TO SHORE. AS JOE AND MOE FIGHT THE INCREASING SWELLS, JENSEN SEES TWO RUBBER BOATS SOME DISTANCE DOWN THE COASTLINE.

YOU BOYS GO HOME. TROUBLE HERE. THANKS!

DRAWING HIS PISTOL, JENSEN MAKES HIS WAY TOWARD THE GUNFIRE. HE SEES SEVERAL SOLDIERS WHO CLEARLY AREN'T JAPANESE AND APPROACHES THEM CAUTIOUSLY.

YOU A COASTWATCHER?

NO. I'M A PAN AM PILOT WHO ESCAPED FROM THE JAPANESE.